JOSEPH MIDTHUN   SAMUEL HITI

BUILDING BLOCKS OF SCIENCE

CELLS TO ORGAN SYSTEMS

WORLD BOOK

a Scott Fetzer company
Chicago
www.worldbook.com

World Book, Inc.
233 N. Michigan Avenue
Chicago, IL 60601
U.S.A.

For information about other World Book publications,
visit our website at www.worldbook.com
or call 1-800-WORLDBK (967-5325).
For information about sales to schools and libraries,
call 1-800-975-3250 (United States),
or 1-800-837-5365 (Canada).

Library of Congress Cataloging-in-Publication Data

Cells to organ systems.
        pages cm. -- (Building blocks of science)
     Summary: "A graphic nonfiction volume that
introduces the cells, tissues, and organs of the
human body"-- Provided by publisher.
    Includes index.
    ISBN 978-0-7166-1841-6
    1. Life (Biology)--Juvenile literature. 2. Organs
(Anatomy)--Juvenile literature. 3. Cells--Juvenile
literature. I. World Book, Inc.
    QH501.C376 2014
    571.6--dc23
                                    2013024687

Building Blocks of Science
ISBN: 978-0-7166-1840-9 (set, hc.)

Printed in China by Shenzhen Donnelley
Printing Co., Ltd., Guangdong Province
2nd printing January 2015

Acknowledgments:
Created by Samuel Hiti and Joseph Midthun
Art by Samuel Hiti
Written by Joseph Midthun
Special thanks to Syril McNally

TABLE OF CONTENTS

There is a glossary on page 30. Terms defined in the glossary are in type **that looks like this** on their first appearance.

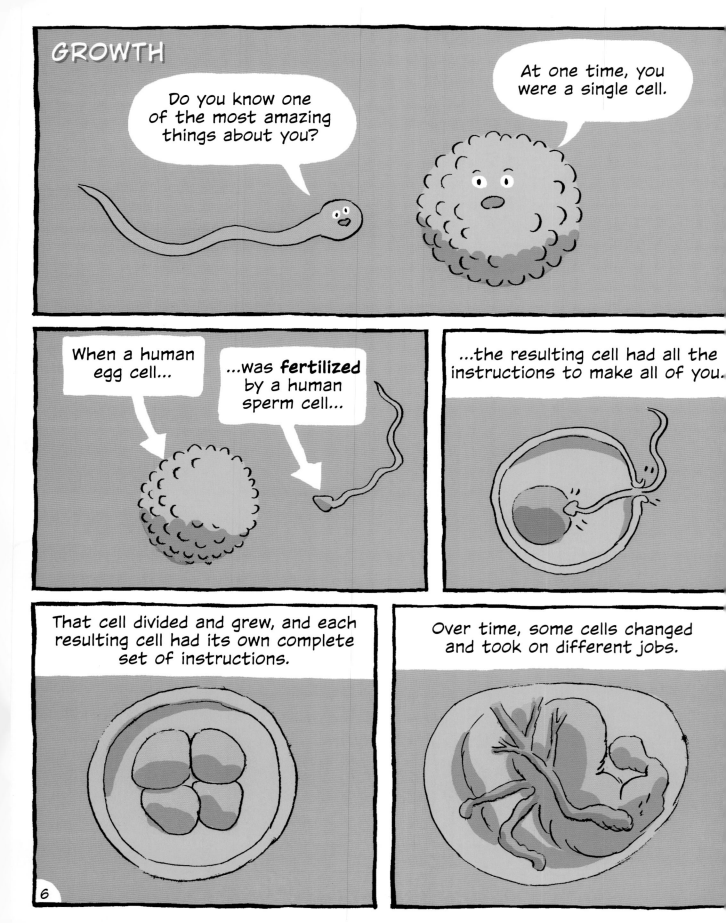

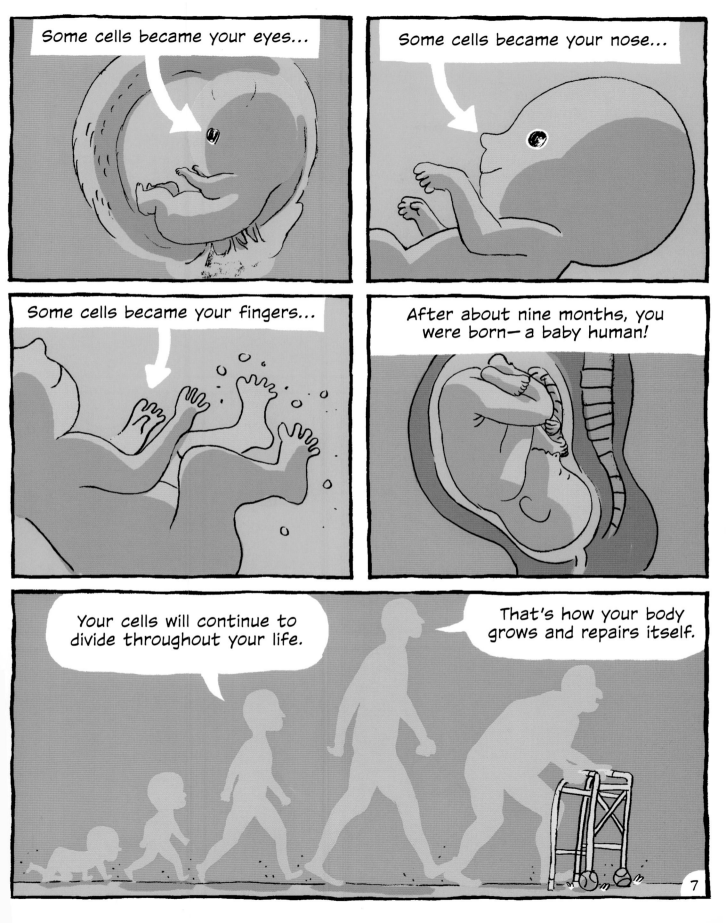

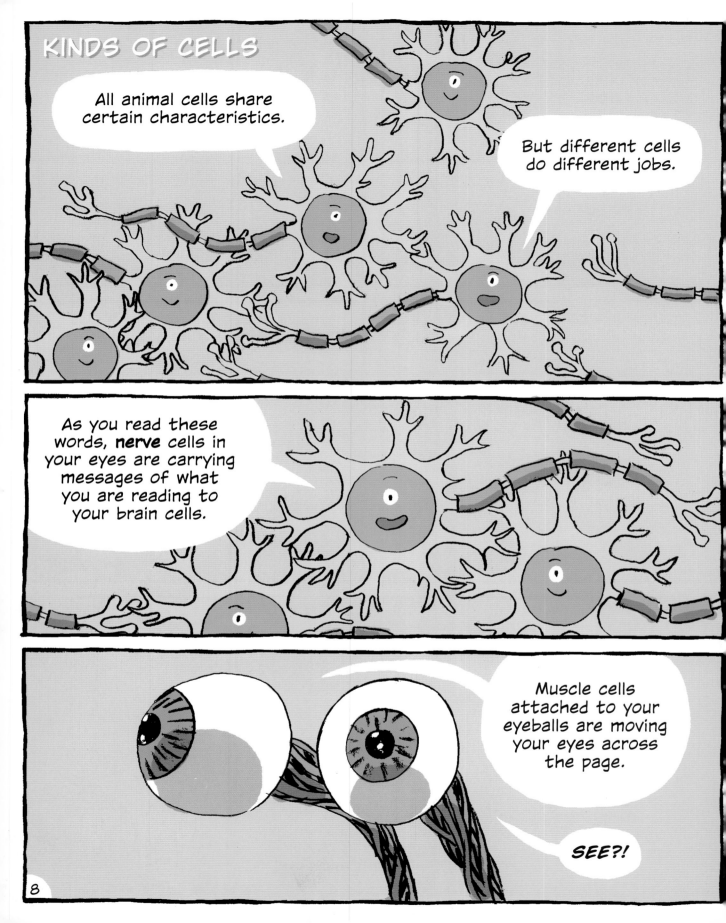

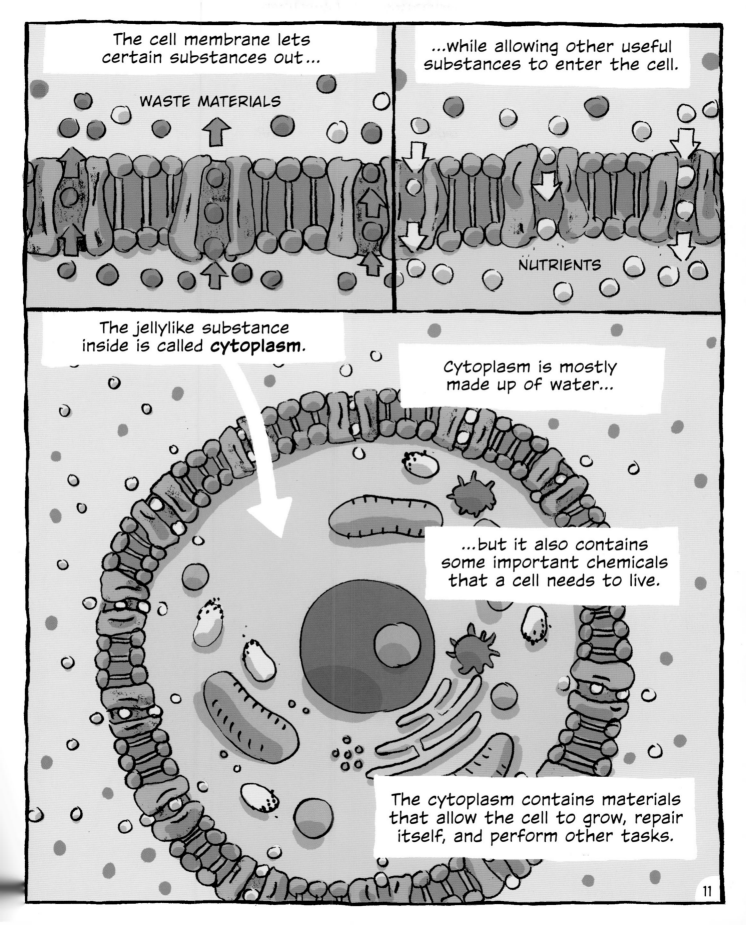

The cell membrane lets certain substances out...

WASTE MATERIALS

...while allowing other useful substances to enter the cell.

NUTRIENTS

The jellylike substance inside is called **cytoplasm**.

Cytoplasm is mostly made up of water...

...but it also contains some important chemicals that a cell needs to live.

The cytoplasm contains materials that allow the cell to grow, repair itself, and perform other tasks.

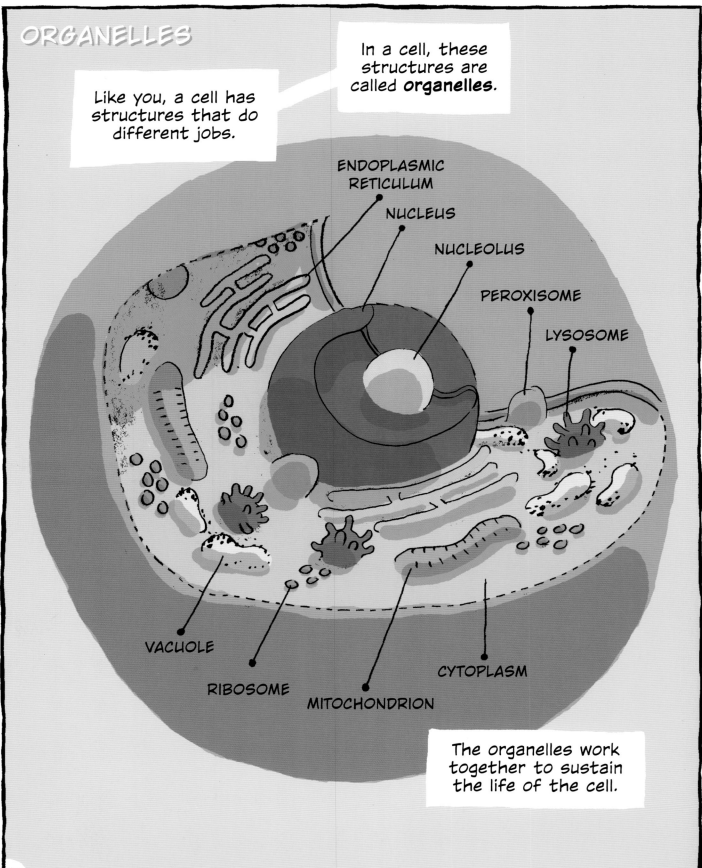

Mitochondria are another kind of organelle.
We convert the chemical energy from the food you consume...
...into a form of energy the cell can use to grow, divide, and do its job.

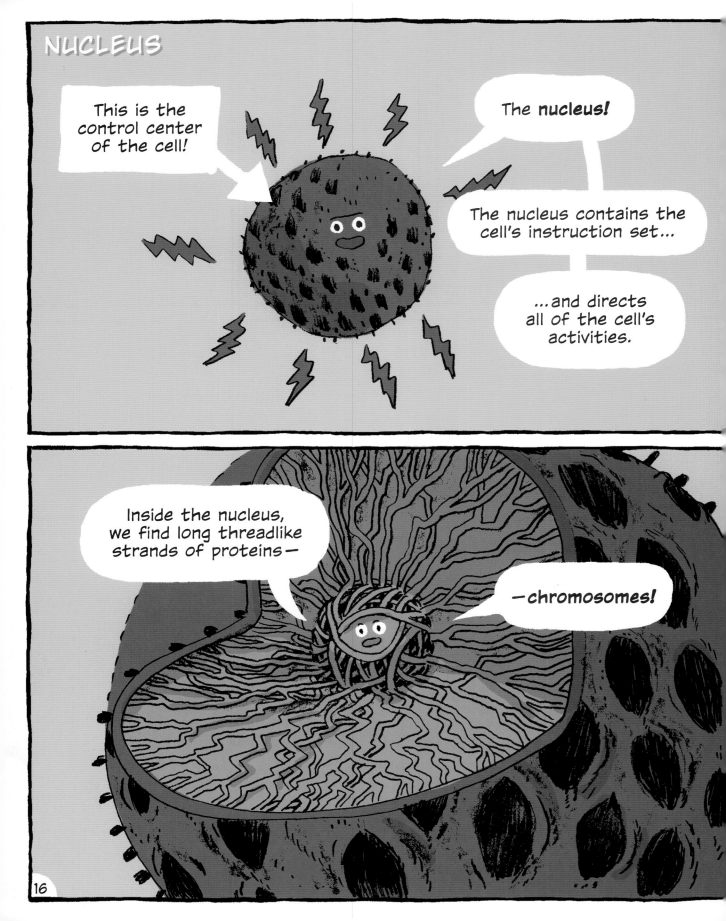

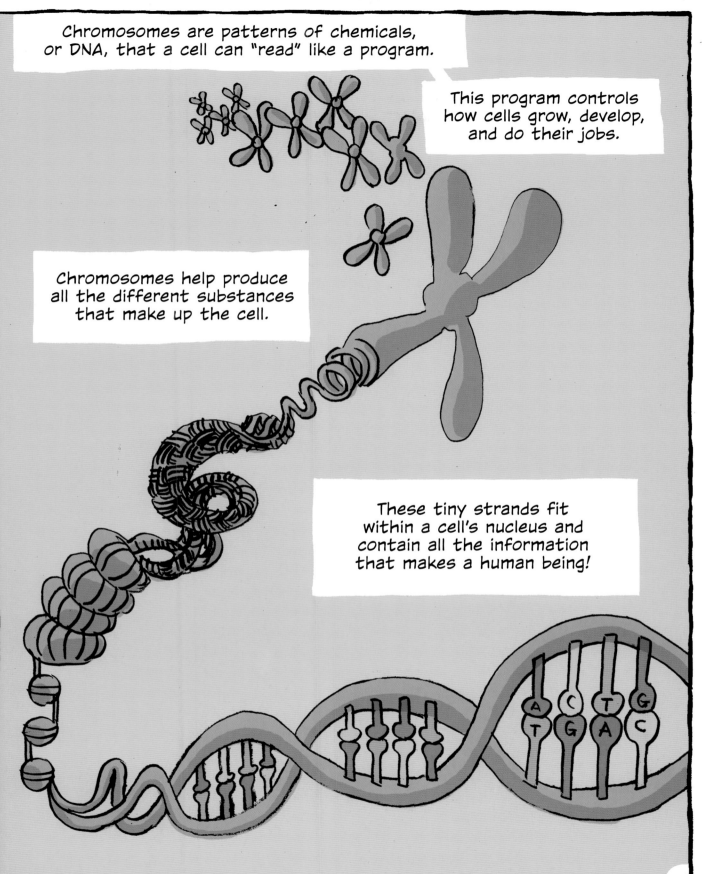

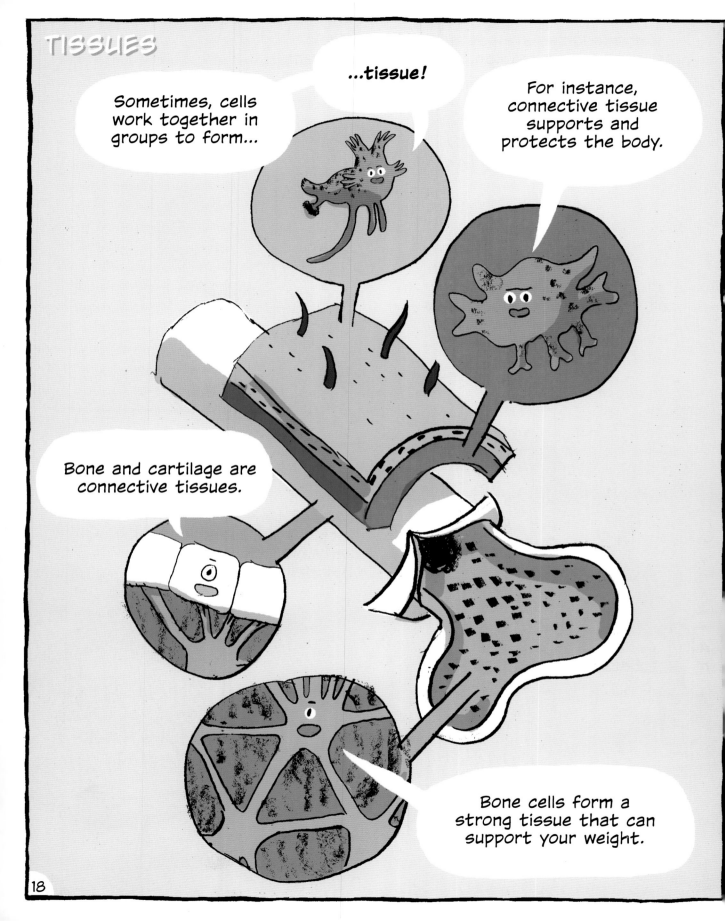

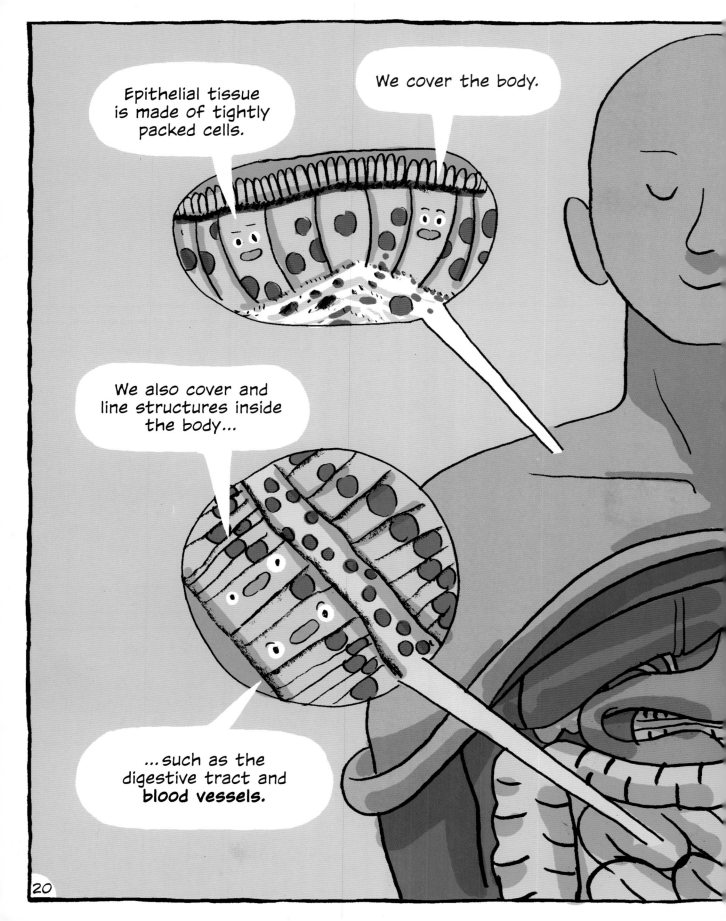

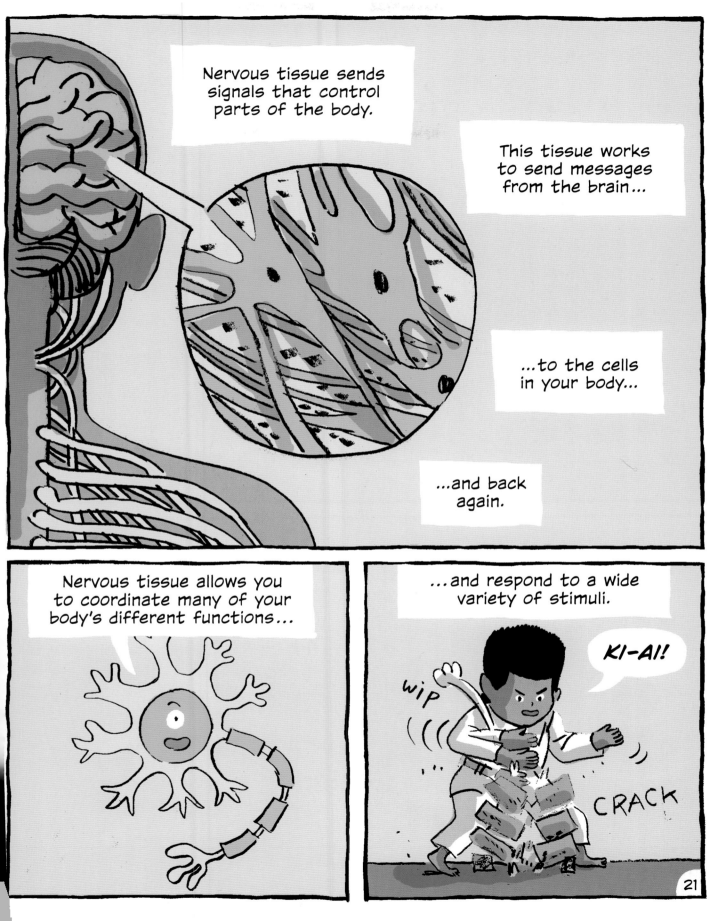

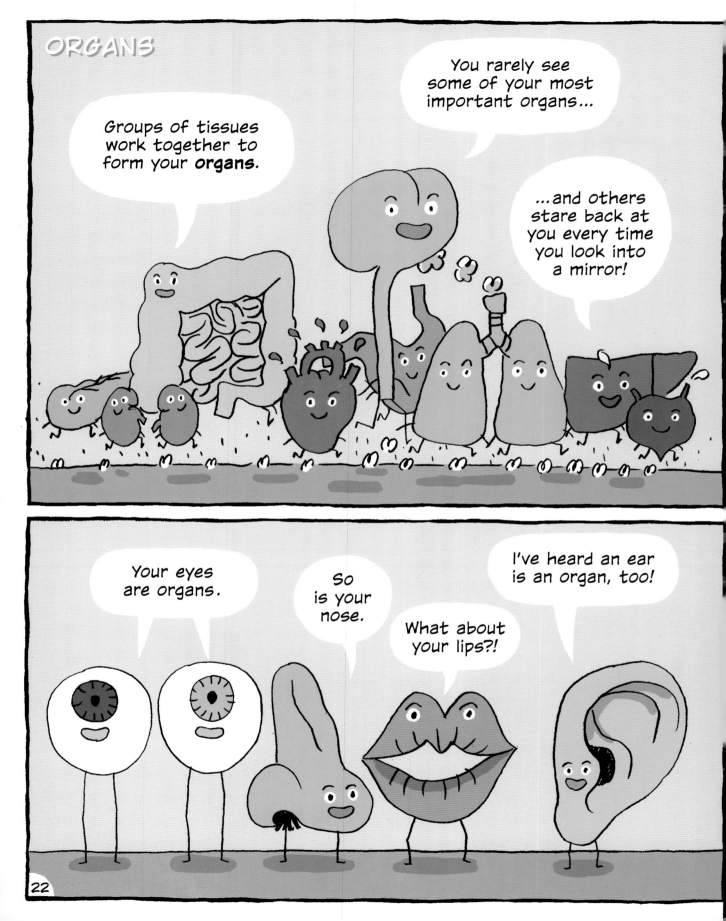

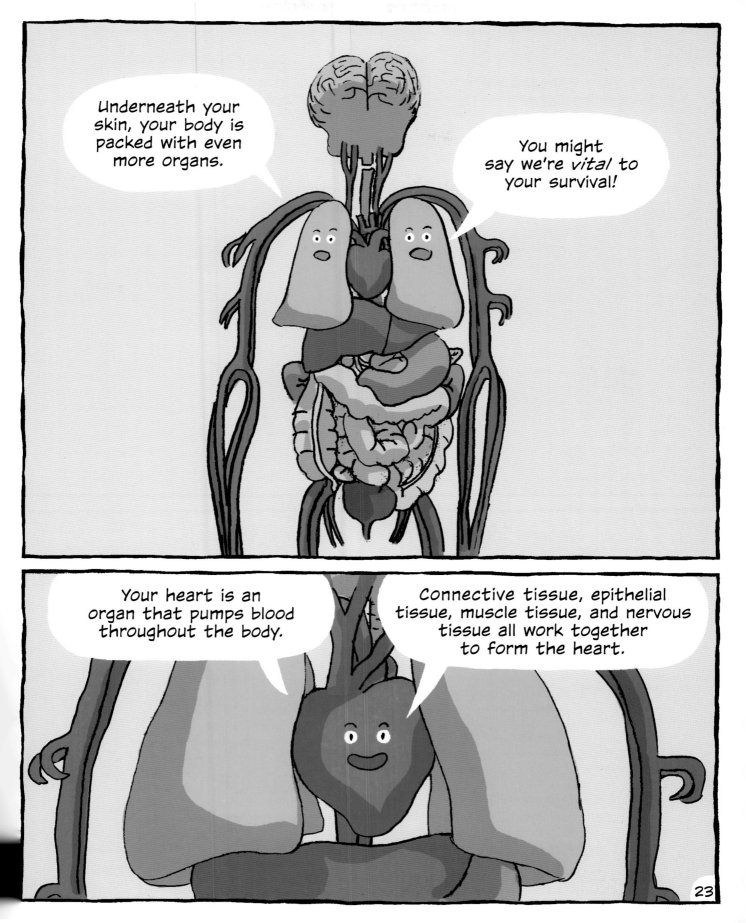

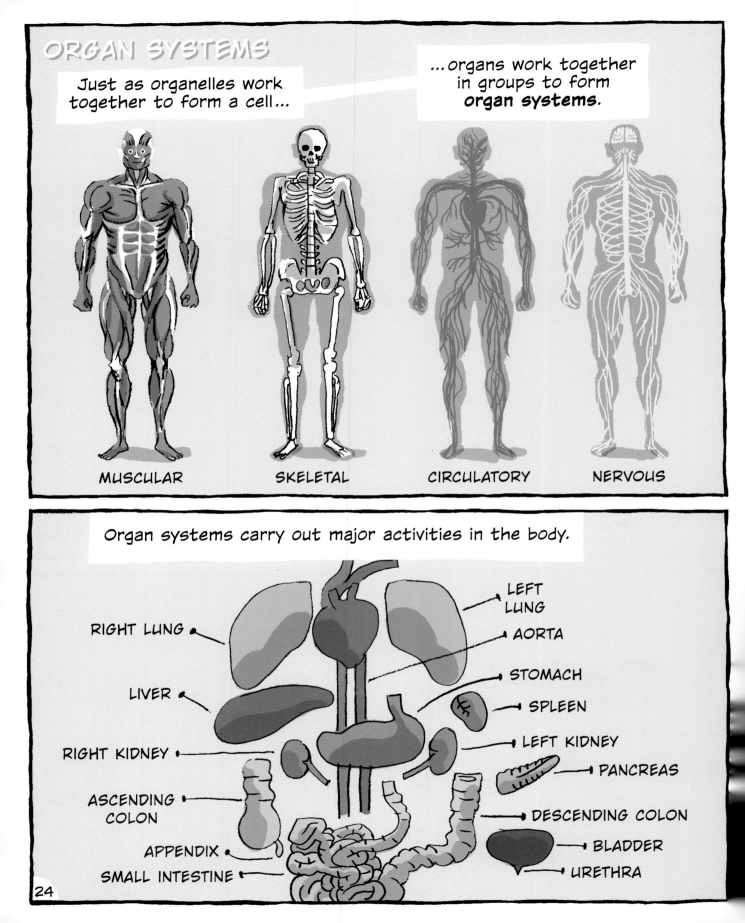

ORGAN SYSTEMS

Just as organelles work together to form a cell...

...organs work together in groups to form **organ systems**.

MUSCULAR

SKELETAL

CIRCULATORY

NERVOUS

Organ systems carry out major activities in the body.

RIGHT LUNG

LEFT LUNG

AORTA

LIVER

STOMACH

SPLEEN

RIGHT KIDNEY

LEFT KIDNEY

PANCREAS

ASCENDING COLON

DESCENDING COLON

APPENDIX

BLADDER

SMALL INTESTINE

URETHRA

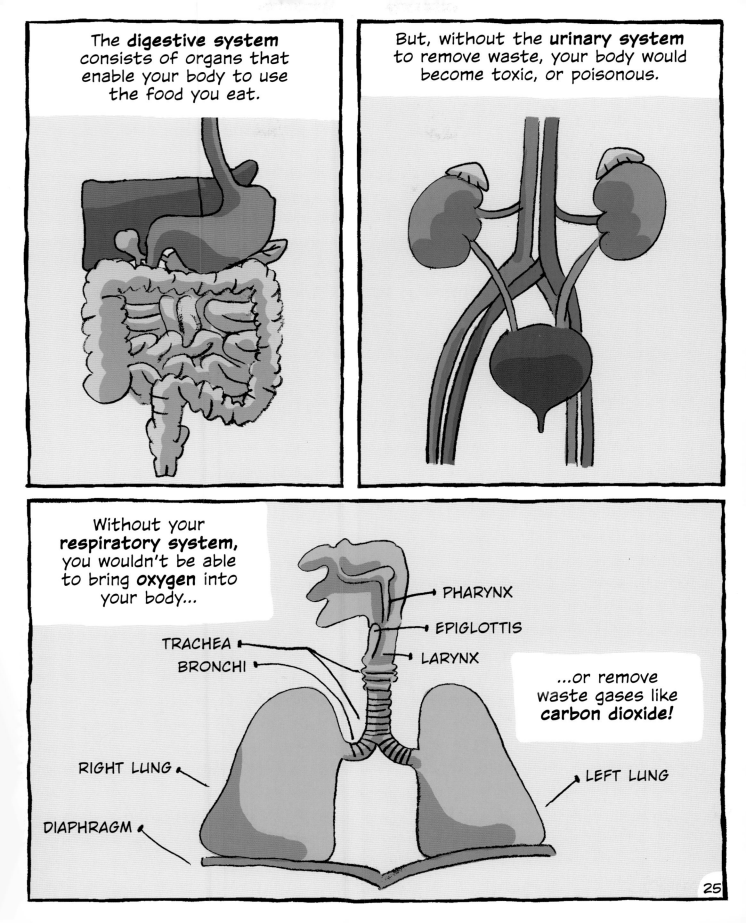

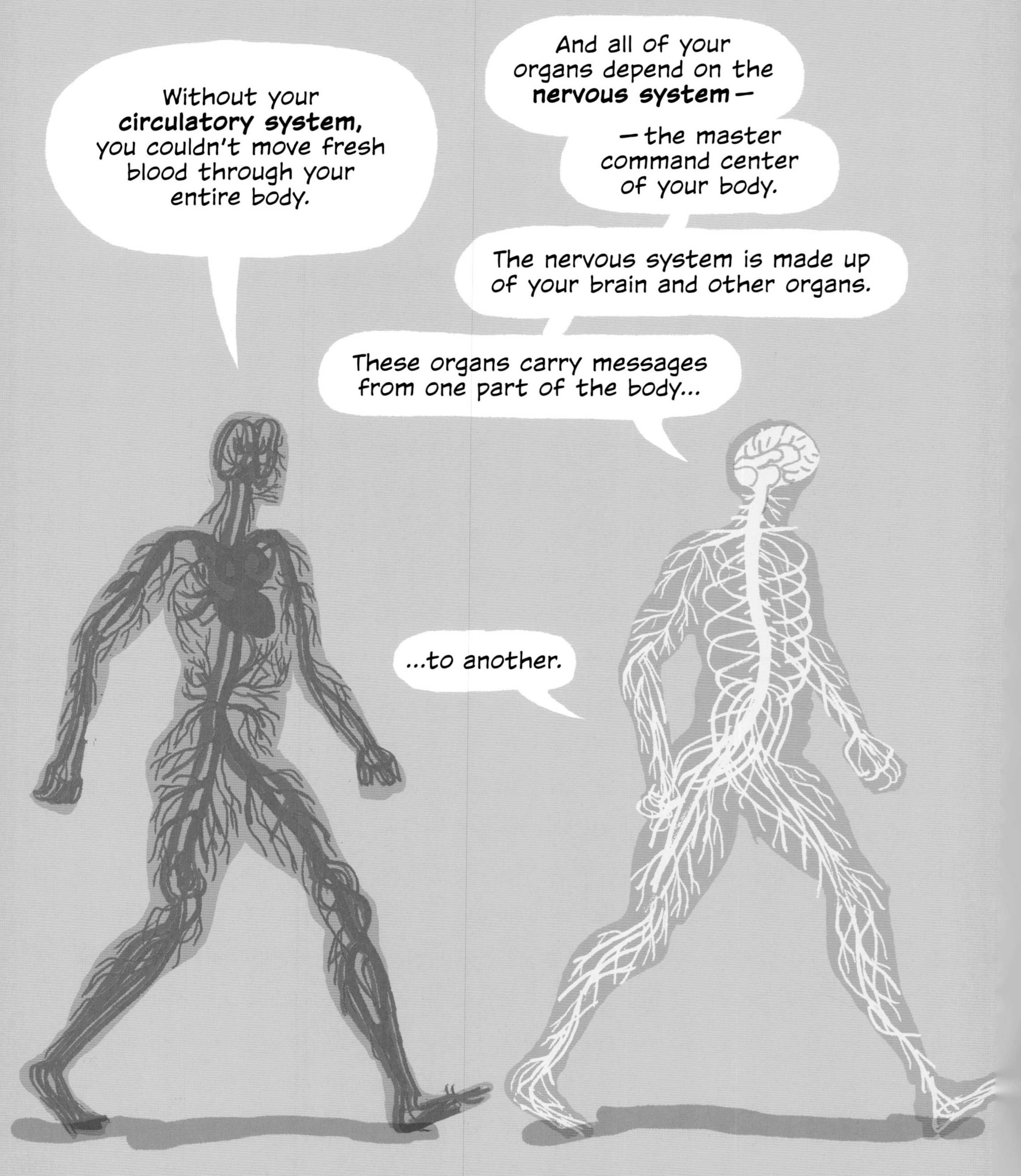
Without your **circulatory system,** you couldn't move fresh blood through your entire body.
And all of your organs depend on the **nervous system** —
— the master command center of your body.
The nervous system is made up of your brain and other organs.
These organs carry messages from one part of the body...
...to another.

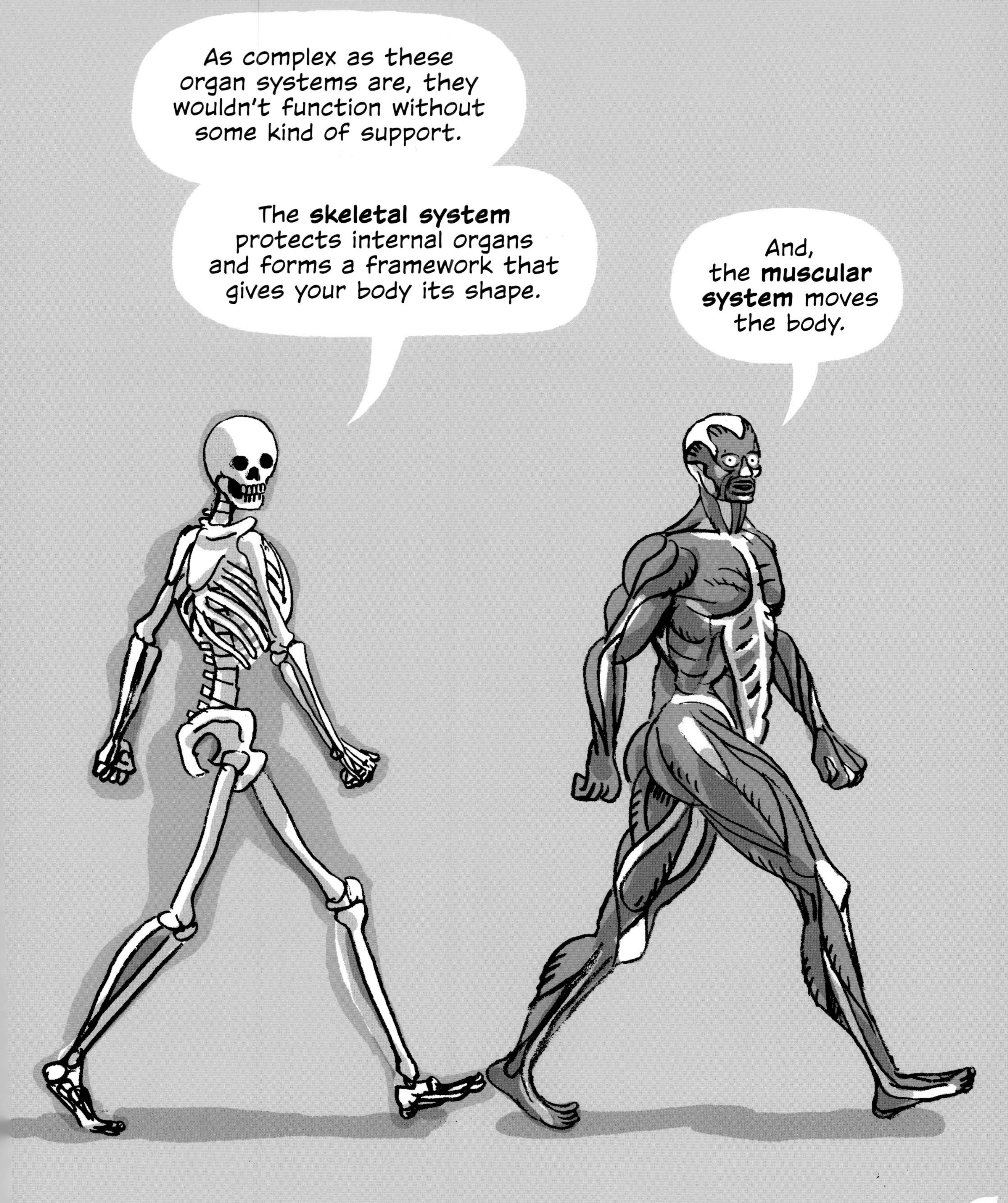
As complex as these organ systems are, they wouldn't function without some kind of support.
The **skeletal system** protects internal organs and forms a framework that gives your body its shape.
And, the **muscular system** moves the body.

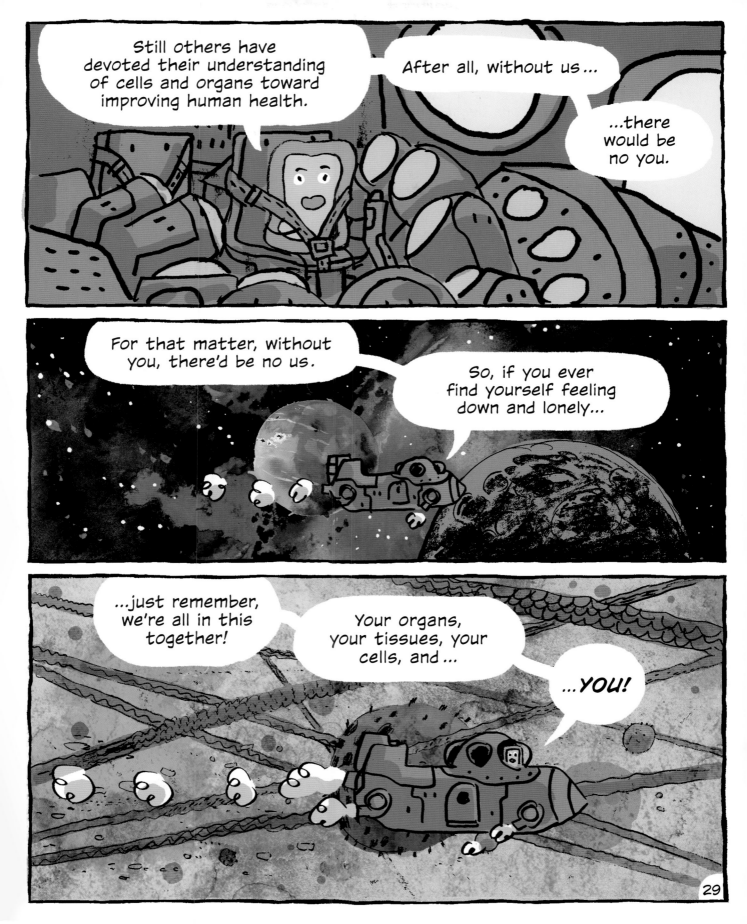

GLOSSARY

bacterium; bacteria a tiny single-celled organism; more than one bacterium.

blood vessel a hollow tube that carries blood and nutrients through the body.

carbon dioxide the air that is breathed out of the lungs.

cell the basic unit of all living things.

cell membrane a covering that separates the inside of a cell from the outside environment.

chromosome threadlike strands that direct cell activity.

circulatory system the group of organs that carries blood through the body.

cytoplasm the material that fills a cell.

digestive system the group of organs that breaks down and absorbs food in the body.

fertilize the process by which a male sperm cell and a female egg cell join together.

mitochondrion; mitochondria the "power plant" of a cell; more than one mitochondrion.

muscular system all of the muscles that cover the bones and move the body.

nerve a bundle of fibers that connects body parts and sends messages in the body.

nervous system the group of nerves and organs that controls all activities in the body.

nucleus the "control center" of a cell.

nutrient a food substance that helps body growth.

organ two or more tissues that work together to do a certain job.

organ system two or more organs that do a common task.

organelle an organlike structure within the cell that has a specific job.

oxygen an essential gas that is breathed into the lungs.

respiratory system the group of organs that brings oxygen into the body and removes carbon dioxide.

skeletal system the entire collection of bones and tissues in the body.

tissue a group of similar cells that do a certain job.

urinary system the group of organs that removes wastes from the blood.

vacuole a small storage space in a cell.

FIND OUT MORE

Books

Cells, Tissues, and Organs
by Donna Latham
(Raintree, 2009)

Hear Your Heart
by Paul Showers
(HarperCollins, 2000)

Human Body
by Richard Walker
(DK Children, 2009)

Human Body Factory: The Nuts and Bolts of Your Insides
by Dan Green
(Kingfisher, 2012)

Repairing and Replacing Organs
by Andrew Solway
(Heinemann, 2008)

The Way We Work
by David Macaulay
(Houghton Mifflin/Walter Lorraine Books, 2008)

Tissues, Organs, and Systems
by Karen Bledsoe
(Perfection Learning, 2007)

Ultra-Organized Cell Systems
by Rebecca L. Johnson
(Lerner Classroom, 2007)

Websites

Biology 4 Kids: Cell Structure
http://www.biology4kids.com/files/cell_main.html
Get an in-depth education on all of the parts that make up a cell.

Kids Biology: Biology of Cells, Tissues, Organs, Organ Systems, and Organisms
http://www.kidsbiology.com/biology_basics/cells_tissues_organs/structure_of_living_things1.php
Learn all about the cells, tissues, and organs that make up your body systems by watching short videos and reading fun, fact-filled articles.

Kids Health: How the Body Works
http://kidshealth.org/kid/htbw/
Select a body part to watch a video, play a word find, or read an article to learn more about its function in the human body.

Kids Konnect: The Human Body
http://www.kidskonnect.com/subjectindex/31-educational/health/337-human-body.html
Tickle your brain with some fascinating fast facts about the body's many systems.

Kids.Net.Au: Biological Cell
http://encyclopedia.kids.net.au/page/bi/Biological_cell
All of your questions about your body's cells will be answered in this detailed article.

NeoK12: Cell Structures
http://www.neok12.com/Cell-Structures.htm
Watch videos that illustrate the structure of cells, and then take grade-specific quizzes to test your knowledge.

Science Kids: Human Body for Kids
http://www.sciencekids.co.nz/humanbody.html
Sample a range of educational games, challenging experiments, and mind-bending quizzes, all while learning about human body topics.

INDEX